BEFORE
I HAD
THE WORD

TEXAS REVIEW PRESS • HUNTSVILLE, TEXAS

BEFORE
I HAD
THE WORD

POEMS

BROOKE SAHNI

Copyright

Library of Congress
Cataloging-in-Publication Data
Name: Sahni, Brooke, author.
Title: Before I had the word : poems / Brooke Sahni.
Description: Huntsville : Texas Review Press, [2021]
"2020 Winner of the X. J. Kennedy Poetry Prize."–Page 65, ECIP galley.
Identifiers: LCCN 2021017002 (print) | LCCN 2021017003 (ebook) |
ISBN 9781680032574 (paperback) | ISBN 9781680032581 (ebook)
Subjects: LCSH: Immanence of God–Poetry. | LCGFT: Poetry.
Classification: LCC PS3619.A3935 B44 2021 (print) |
LCC PS3619.A3935 (ebook) | DDC 811/.6–dc23
LC record available at https://lccn.loc.gov/2021017002
LC ebook record available at https://lccn.loc.gov/2021017003
Original cover art by Solange Roberdeau, *Tree Sight (4)*, 2016
Cover Design: Bradley Alan Ivey | Interior Design: PJ Carlisle
Printed in the United States of America
Published by Texas Review Press
texasreviewpress.org
Huntsville, Texas
77341

2020 Winner of The X. J. Kennedy Poetry Prize

Established in 1998, The X. J. Kennedy Prize highlights one full-length collection of poetry per year.

Previous Winners:

Caroline M. Mar, *Special Education*

Garret Keizer, *The World Pushes Back*

Jay Udall, *Because a Fire in Our Heads*

Jeff Hardin, *No Other Kind of World*

Gwen Hart, *The Empress of Kisses*

Corinna McClanahan Schroeder, *Inked*

Ashley Mace Havird, *The Garden of the Fugitives*

Jeff Worley, *A Little Luck*

James McKean, *We Are the Bus*

George Drew, *The View from Jackass Hill*

Joshua Coben, *Maker of Shadows*

Ashley Renee, *Basic Heart*

William Baer, *"Bocage" and Other Sonnets*

Becky Gould Gibson, *Aphrodite's Daughter*

Deborah Bogen, *Landscape with Silos*

Lee Rudolph, *A Woman and a Man, Ice-Fishing*

Eric Nelson, *Terrestrials*

Jan Lee Ande, Reliquary

Jorn Ake, *Asleep in the Lightning Fields*

Barbara Lau, *The Long Surprise*

Philip Heldrich, *Good Friday*

Gray Jacobik, *The Surface of Last Scattering*

Contents

1   Before I had the word

2   *Sikh* Coming from the Punjabi Meaning *Disciple* or *Seeker*

3   G-d, a Portrait

4   *Mangifera Indica*

5   Language Lesson

6   Heritage Day

7   Leaving a Scripture

8   How to Build a Body

10   Notes on Midrash

15   Lore

16   Natural Law

17   Divine Law

18   *The Sensuous Woman* by J

19   In your girlhood

20   Order

21   Creation Myth

22   To the girl who cried over grass

23   Whose Kingdom

What My Mother Knows   24

Divining   25

Reform   26

Notes on Midrash   30

Jettison   34

The Body of the Guru   42

Why I ask for you to come in dreams   43

What We Believed   44

On Absence   45

Notes on the Amorphous   46

After Watching *Religulous* With a Friend   47

Book Arts   48

Inflorescence   50

Casting, Pulling   51

If you took out the *e*, you could be like the stream 52

Ritual, Begging   53

The Golden Reserve   54

Acknowledgments   56

Before I had the word

I was placed in the center
of the crib,
ushered to sleep before sunfall—
that strange occupation
of infancy,
those endless surrenders.
This is how I came
to know you:
all fragment, light, quivering
shapes on the carpet,
aluminum blinds casting golden
runners on the walls,
the small globes above me
duplicating worlds on my skin—

I didn't need the word,
hadn't learned to omit the *o*
from your spelling,
its round plushcore
like abundance, satiation,
and inconsequential
in the way my own infant skin
rounded out toward
what I could not touch,
the fat, the golden reserve
essential until it wasn't—
we say that fat is burned,
as if singed, removed,
O, holy body,
what you no longer need
refuses to exit,
burrows,
shrunken and dormant.

Sikh Coming from the Punjabi Meaning *Disciple* or *Seeker*

The English root of *Sikh*
is *seek, learn* or *study*

>   for years, I thought
>   to be a *disciple* meant I must grow

down into a small
thing—there was no seeking

>   just s*urrender*

our teachers didn't tell us
the root of *siddur* stems from

>   *order*
>   *order* so unlike *devotion*

but assigned each of us a tree,
I met mine in spring

>   buds still shy
>   *ulmus rubra*

slippery elm—
the root of a plant absorbs

G-d, a Portrait

First, we were taught how to spell
His name, then we were told to draw Him.
It was an exercise in metaphor.
The balls of paper amassed before me
while my classmates drew stars, maps of the Holy Land.
I thought I should color everything I could think of
knowing—human hands, the golden breakfast yolk,
thick-skinned tree—knowing somewhere it was all correct.
Writing *g-o-d* in the corner of the page, discarding it,
and still everything remained the same.
Then the desecrated flower, drawn out
in parts: stem, petal, stamen, pollen, even a bee to operate,
because between the third and the seventh,
it all happened so suddenly—where god
was impatient I took my time.
Outside new plants went on growing
as we sat in our huddles, trying to draw
something.

Mangifera Indica

If he hadn't been an illegal immigrant, my uncle, a great

    brown bulb, might have flourished, emerged,

        untangled himself, instead of rising only when called,

climbing the old stairs to his mother, my grandmother, in the kitchen

        weaving my hair. Or if *success* had little to do

with *absence,* my dad small among his boxes, might have left the backyard sorting

    merchandise and descended to the basement

        with a loving cup of tea, each brother confessing,

    yes, it's been a long day, or, when the moon

was whole, the brothers might have met on the patio

    to reminisce about their backyard mango tree in Delhi,

        the one they each told me about but never

at the same time, so I had to braid their stories,

    grow my own epic mango tree. I imagine the way my grandmother

   used her hands to peel the flesh from the meat so the boys could plant the pit.

If my father called down, my uncle called up, we could have, all of us,

    gathered in the living room and spoke.

The three of them could have taught mom and me

        Hindi words, beginning with the most essential:

hello and *nice to see you.*

Language Lesson

There are fields beyond the glass window,
they appear to ripple and writhe. To pass time
my uncle teaches me what *mirage* means,

how in India everything undulates, so hot
you can cook an egg on the street. Now I see
it's not the fields that are moving, but a hovering

light. I am too young to conceptualize the soul—
what I mean is, I don't think about metaphor.
There are green fields with an illusion

so close to the skin, they are almost one body.
My uncle says, within two months of arriving in America
a man called him *sand nigger*—

I am too young to hold the meaning, just the resonance
of sound. Now I know there are deserts so hot
the sand can strip paint off of the cars,
words that give and words that take away.

Heritage Day

Season of make believe,
I attune myself to forms I see in the movies—
all month teenagers break
into different skins,
witches depart toward night.
I've watched the trees behind the garage,
the yellowing leaves so thin
they appear cut
of willow glass, neither here
nor there.
I make predictions: in two days
the leaves will redden,
in a week they'll fall, depart.

At the mall, my friends and I don't discuss
Heritage Day, instead spend hours among
aisles of wigs, manufactured
blood and fog. Horror or cute? they ask.

Later, the choice: to go Jewish
or Indian. *Sikh* my mom corrects—
that word gone dormant, absent
because my father was,
seek like how I used to write it
in my journal as if to claim it,
as if I would seek and ultimately find.
I descend into the basement to
the clothes kept in the clear bag,
the technicolor womb buried beneath
holiday decorations.
In the light of the living room
I don't feel right in the sari—*heritage* as mercurial
as my reflection. Sikh or Jewish?
Or the one I most admire—ghost,
with its simple palette,
unadorned body.

Leaving a Scripture

Some days,
my teacher slips,
says there is only one god,
that we are *chosen people* as though
god is a ghost and we,
his haunting.
What about that other scripture,
the one that rests high on the shelf
of my closet, like a sleeping animal
with dust on its coat?
From me a thin cord extends,
travels the miles home—slips
in under the door and goes
to the *Guru Granth Sahib*—
you told me,
holy books like this
must be elevated,
left me
with an object
holy and unintelligible.

Though you moved away,
though you say you're not that far,
there is a hush in the house that
lives. But there are words
to describe *jettison,*
thank god for that.

How to Build a Body

When did you come into being? When you were written?

Or when you were sung?

When you were bound?

Or when you were embellished?

When you were dressed?

Or when you were illuminated?

Torah, they say you are holy

And they call you the body of the guru

There's a way to read myself—

But can't you see their eyes when they read us?

True, what wild surrender

They touch me with a silver hand
too sacred to touch, prone toward
blur

They light my pages with gold paint
gold hammered down, thinned, mixed
with stag's glue

Illuminated sounds like *enlightened*—
once I could see through sunlit fields,
I was animal—an ox, sheep, deer,
lamb

My colored ink, the devoted hand—meaning steady

My ink originates from tree sap, honey, gall—but—always black
304,805 letters inscribed, my scribe cannot
use an iron pen, iron is leashed to violence—

But aren't your pages are filled with violence? What does that do to a person?

You see my robe and crown?

                                        I see you curled in scroll

Your rainbow-edged pages, 6,000 line compositions

                                        You ornate, holy thing

I don't know—they undress me like a woman,
            kiss me when I fall
objects to be used

                                                        Sing me

Sing me

            They raise me on their altar, prayers for milestones, death,
        birth, marriage, when I hear myself sung it feels so unlike myself,
            my body, not my body, voices to articulate me onward

What does it feel like for your words to be
            unaltered?

                                        I told you I am sung with nuance in the pitch

I didn't hear you

                                                        So listen

You don't sound like god

                                        I could say the same for you

Notes on Midrash

1.

Sex ed. came early, arrived in the form of having us gather in a circle to ask. But first the teacher held up diagrams, unholy-ed the body with mechanics—*ovum, tubes, minora* and *majora*. I don't remember any mention of pleasure, and I didn't ask—(the first time I touched myself the elm flowered and I never considered the two blooms as an answer. The question was, *Is pleasure a sacred act?*) The teacher held up a tampon, passed it like *besamim,* asked us if we knew what it was and when Arielle guessed the tampon was a candle the room lit with laughter, I joined, knowing what it was, feeling somehow, the inner ache that awaited me and the teacher said something about the body needing to ready itself in order to receive, so I considered my fingers and how far I would need to root until something broke.

2.

By now I know the hand is holy, it can perform so many tricks. But there is a law that says my skin and the scripture's skin is a sacrilegious contact—why would god make an object that can't be touched when, already, I've touched so many beautiful things? I'll hold the yad for fun, but never recite from the Torah in any formal way—the parents and teachers are disappointed I don't want to become a Bat Mitzvah, a woman in god's eyes, even though it was years before when they let us loose in the woods for an entire weekend and the landscape told me truth that no hands or words will ever touch—

and in the woods they hand us a thick packet of questions. How to Identify a Tree by Its Parts: *1. Students should find plant specimens of their choice, or as specified by you, to identify* . . . but I've brought with me a separate notebook, one I hide among layers of clothes. At night I turn my headlamp on to witness my tiny, secret scrawl. The popular girl's body—how many ways to metaphor the breast? Bud, budding, a flower— the body's stalk? *2. They should observe the main structures of the plant.* The camp counselor takes a group of us on a hike, while our teachers stay behind. It rained last night—we slide, muddy ourselves, and after, in the cafeteria, he removes the slender bar from his tongue, shows us how water can squirt through. In the packet, I describe the forest in spring—muddied, wet, buds. *3. They should try to identify the plant by its fruits or flowers (if not present, continue to step 5). Note the flower's color, shape, size, and cluster type.* I press leaves in-between thick glossed pages of books, and at night I try to write about the counselor, the hole in his tongue.

4.

By the time I am fifteen, I wanted more than I'd ever wanted. I removed the mattress from my room, and didn't miss it, my body so in flux. For years I slept with blankets and books in a giant heap on the ground, which meant maybe I hadn't ever left the *interpretive act of* midrash—*I don't care if we erase the word* ~~god~~—*it's overused and you can roll it around in your mouth until it's absent. I read that mysticism means absorption into the deity, attained through self-surrender*—I wrote this in a high school journal, but mainly the entries began with a boy who visited me in my nest of blankets and books, his touch, the answer.

5.

In teaching us that questioning The Word is sacred, one could say that every question is sacred. A child, I could not wrap my head around many things, a bookmark, for instance, or how a book could contain so many pages one would need to mark it. I asked my mom and she told me sometimes we can't obtain the knowledge all in one sitting.

Lore

in the cabin to the left   a boy   ejaculating into

                                      a plastic bag—a blue one

an important part

             of the story   the news took, split us   in two: those who
                                           understood
                                                    and those who didn't

a few girls   crossed the river to the left

                         the boys anticipated this   one threw the bag at a girl

our Hebrew teacher gathered us

we climbed the bunks   and I swear   the girls who knew
                        took the top   dangled

                                limbs   open   those who

didn't
low and fearful seated on the floor   in a broken tongue   our teacher
taught   what it means to self-

                              serve

and the boys would be punished   Later, the girl cried,

I never realized how easy it is to get pregnant

                     an immaculate seed

had been planted.

Natural Law

She calls it *heartdrum*. It's the Sabbath
and we're sick of talking about god, lighting candles,

saying prayers over wine we're too young
to taste. She sings out an ecstatic, *Da dum. Da dum.*

We light incense, pretend it's a cigarette, dare one another
to kiss the mirror. *Have you ever touched yourself?*

We dip our hands into the candy bowl,
toss the sweets at her. Someone else finds a drum, beats it—

the basement TV emits secular light, illuminates our forms.
In the movie the boy reaches for the white folds of a girl's thigh

and doesn't stop—there is an opening in us, too.
My friends fill the mouth of their sleeping bags, then

I find a plastic tambourine, shake it—
you're like Miriam! they cry,

ash from the cigarette burning my hand.
Even here, in this low cellar,

we cannot separate god,
or this prophet-woman from our pleasure.

Divine Law

    The four of us chase the water spreading over the lawn,
each step drawing roots from grass to heel. One asks, midair,

    What do Jews believe? and suddenly, all I can remember of
my religious education is the way I watched the bough

    reach for the classroom window as if wanting to break inside.
I make the three of them sit in a circle and teach them

    that Joni Mitchell song, the one about the seasons,
and circles, because the song reminds me of summer camp

    and camp reminds me of the woods going so far
back I am certain there is no end.

The Sensuous Woman by J

A woman gets eaten

        out   by a tiger   and the unnamed   author assures

the readers   that this fantasy   is perfectly   natural—

    natural   that a woman might want to   be

tiger *and*

woman—satiated in either form.   We'd found the book in my mother's old

high school dresser   among

yearbooks   photos   diaries   locks   of my baby hair.

    A holy thing   we pass it. Read *rape*   read *pleasure*   read outdated language

—*be the woman every man yearns to make love to—the woman you yearn to be.*

    It's summer

so many things are calling us   into and out of   ourselves   so we close it gently place
 it

back in its darkness   position it

so it looks untouched.

In your girlhood

Miriam was only five years old when she became her mother's helper in delivering Jewish babies, but she was already quite competent.

—Chabad.org

Did you ever complain to your mother,
                    complain about her,
say your prayers, put your shoes on the wrong foot,
                    pretend ghosts in the woods,
punch your brothers,
                    curse god, refuse
vegetables, punish yourself,
                    dream of marriage, play stupid,
play house, play housewife—
                    Five-years-old, did you
fear the female body?
                    The pregnant bulge, the first scream?
Did you even hear the voices,
                    see the water, the well?
Did the voices in your head frighten you?
                    Did the water, cool on your fingertips
temper you,
                    if only for a moment?

Order

O father,
O logic,
you tell me
it's so simple,
the answer
right there, but I may as well be
looking down the throat
of god or the rainstorm
of your language
when you speak it.
You yell, *figure it out now,*
you yell the rules—
there is no guesswork here—
and somewhere the word *stupid*—

There are two gravities of seeing:
one that holds you here
and me beyond what
you cannot see—
where to go but toward
the light bending
behind the trees?
You circle
until the pencil breaks,
the equation on the
page haloed black,
still fractured.

Creation Myth

It had always been there,
a cell curling away from the vein
of my street,
portal of curve and meander,
trees bowing in to each other.
The cul-de-sac. Riding
my green bicycle, I circle,
orchestrate plans involving a future
cul-de-sac civilization,
where each house
would house my friends,
and in the evenings we'd meet
for incandescent bonfires, roast wild
robin meat on the flame, cast offerings
to the sky. Yes, one day I'd live in a cul-de-sac,
be a huntress and forager—men
are not part of my grand scheme—
feather in hair, I'd free all the domestic dogs
to play in the center island of grass,
while I looked down from the rooftop,
yipping. In heat, I ride faster
to the opening that leads
back to the street, dream up
an enclosure of trees,
because a circle
encircles
and that's what makes it so
pleasing.

To the girl who cried over grass

and her steady body planted

like a pot and me,
somewhere between
the ground and the sky.

Me, for once,
tired of being all-earth.
If this is for her, then this is for all
things uprooted,

the human desire
to cultivate.

For each new daily violence,
the ones we
cannot contain any more,
they swell
our tongues.
There was grass,
summer grass, and her
small body crying for what was
being pulled, each *stop*
lifting me from
the ground, *stop*
unearthing
the god in me.

Whose Kingdom

Down the darkened aisles
of your warehouse, you steer me
in your chariot. Past the matte brown,
clear-mouthed, taped-shut towers
of boxes, we glide. Young men
in forklifts wrangle merchandise,
I can see their eyes avert from yours,
see a tremble from within
as they dip their heads, a bow.
Like all good monarchs, you know
how to point: *no, not like that,* or, to me,
he's strong, a rare approval.

It took a lifetime for this galaxy
of imports and silver-backed
machinery to emerge, so you
will understand why I can't
separate you from it. Why sometimes
I try to imagine you as a boy,
the smooth, untouched skin of your feet
at the base of an altar, all bangle,
turban, and simple devotion,
your guru taped behind the thin bars
of your bed that only your slender
wrists could reach
through and touch.

What My Mother Knows

Minutes ago, I tell you
I want to eat a leaf for dinner,
what unplanned response
Buddhists might call *mushin,* or
no thought. It's summer
and our small yard is swollen,
giving. The low-hanging elm leaves
refract edens of light,
my new swing is a lifeline
to the sky. Dipping my head
back up and the returning
blood spins everything godly.
Thanks to you, before me
the large-palmed leaf glistens
on a white plate—my small bite
is bitter, but there is joy—
where god says
forbidden, you say, *eat.*

Divining

The room is full: fire, air, water, and me—all earth.

Years away from sex, we ache.

Last week our kind-of friend, the prophetess, (fire) told us if a girl doesn't shave her pussy,
a boy will never touch her there.

Between her legs, the glossed pages of the magazine, her voice cool as amethyst.

How to give the perfect flavored blowjob; how to remove period stains; how to eat
and not get full;

How simple it is to forget the animal: inside, designer alligator boots; mink coat;
black hide; silkworm spun to paisley.

She finds the horoscope page—the inward waters and I have been waiting for this,
so uncertain of my body, what forms I will take, what sulks beyond this. I,
the only Virgo, make my way down to my back, wait to be divined.

Outside the sky is dark, too distant.

There are no stars.

Reform

If a well is what's hidden, words
are the rope that tried to pull Miriam
from its walls, attempted to reshape
her body into one of relevance, worded
her inner spring, *miracle,*
the phrase I would have used
a decade ago, as in, it would be
a miracle if I ever gave up
my home—its hardwoods, fireflies,
summers of green, and fields of water,
not to mention the neighborhoods
that shaped me: ancient, big-boned
houses, the knowing faces glancing back,
lake effect winters, trudging through
our mutual, seasonal anguish. I would
have said it unlikely to give up
that home for what is now my desert,
a journey that required no grueling pilgrimage,
but a straight line through air,
smooth landing.

I could say that leaving was painful—it was—
there was absence everywhere I looked,
a teacher taught me about the desert flora,
what it looks like to be in need and
what it looks like to be quenched.
Occasionally rain would
come, petrichor lifting from the ground like a ghost,

and I didn't contemplate Miriam's magic

then, nor as child when, once a year,

we danced with timbrels and sang her

song. I was *disciple*, therefore *surrender*—

Now I am learning what it's like to word

the ineffable, like a water-

being-drawn-from-the-center

sensation—a small pain—

I read

Miriam is mentioned in the Torah only a few times

but she made the desert bloom with green

pastures, beautifully scented flowers,

sustained a tribe for forty years—

I read

Miriam's earliest prophecy was that her mother was

going to give birth to a son who would free the Jewish people

from Egyptian bondage. This is one of the reasons why she

was also called Puah, meaning "Whisperer,"

for she was whispering words of prophecy

and part of me takes *whisper* to mean *hesitant*,

a fully quenched thing

living inside, an inner reserve articulated

quietly—or, that when she spoke, everyone

had to lean in to hear her, words so swollen that

when god struck her with leprosy for criticizing her brother,

one might ask: Is language an alchemical act?

Where in the body does language reside?

Why was Miriam punished so harshly?

So we can learn to ask and call the asking holy.

In my desert, I suffer comfortably. Here, from bed,

I can look up philosophical questions,

like why did the Jews wander for forty years?

Wandering is, of course, a metaphor.

After all, what would a straight shot to the Holy Land

do for ones' spiritual evolution?

Say *Jew* and *wander*

and most will say, *desert.*

I remember what seemed the intelligent design

of White Sands, tricking my senses to think: snow.

And low in a valley once, the humbling possibility

of a mountain lion.

Sometimes while hiking, I think, *I miss water,*

then wandering through scrub oak, cholla graveyards,

shards of granite, fields of mesquite,

stumbling through every parched

and dried out specimen,

I find it.

I don't expect The Word to tell me much,

besides, there is metaphor everywhere I look—

mirrorings of meaning, like

Miriam, coming from the Hebrew word for *bitter.*

Ask me not to think of the bitterroot,

purple-petaled flower, named

for its ability to regenerate from dry

seemingly dead roots and no one

calls it *supernatural*, just science.

I knew the desert had taken hold when
my writing turned from green to brown,
something, as always, needed to end so
I can word it *bitterroot* or *reborn*,
death or *Miriam's Well*, *growth*, etc.
What if The Word were a book of botany,

a seduction of plants,

so when I reached the bitterroot,

I saw *plant* and *woman*,
I read, *regenerate*, and read about the people,
the animals that tendrilled from her trunk,
far reaching taproot—
there are books that mean, *scripture*.
Miriam are you real?
Are you metaphor?
I do not want a wrathful god.
I want you so we could walk out
on tonight's vernal swell,
 saying yes, *magic*, yes *divine*,
 certainly *miraculous*, that we could
stand together,
 not word any of it.

Notes on Midrash

6.

Why must we question in order to lead a religious life? I never think of a religious life as anything but, and it takes practice to try to say so. For instance, before college we spent three weeks in the woods, and three of those days alone. I thought those days would be my holy days—solitude, time lapping slowly forward. I chose to fast because god recognizes those who fast—I wanted to be in my body more. I got naked under the sun—I was hungry—and thought the sun would feed me, but there were so many flies buzzing, I couldn't absorb anything. I had never seen so many and after three, four, ten hours, I grew loneliness out of hunger and flies. I dressed myself and tried to write, but all I wrote about were the flies. When that was finished and I still had days ahead of me, I killed one and took its pieces apart—transparent wing, compound eye, antennae—I pressed the parts in my notebook and wondered what night would bring and if the flies would return. I labeled the collection of parts "on trying to be in the light and failing."

7.

The story had articulated anew inside my mother—the stranger at the playground who dug a finger inside, my great-grandmother standing on the sidelines, unseeing. My mother says she wishes she could have been there to mother her mother, wishes that she had the words to fill the absence. And I sit there listening, considering the stranger who could have taken my grandmother to any darkened corner, the inward tunnel children like to climb through, or the elm's private shadow, how instead he lifted her, skyward.

8.

In the poem, there is a hunting scene and my student says it's the first poem he's liked all semester because the language feels masculine. Is language gendered? I ask my students. What to call *flowers*, say, or *violence*. I dispute my student, say, anyone can write poetry and, what does it mean to be masculine in writing? In reality, deep in a drawer rests a poem of my own about the time my partner knifed into the doe on the side of the road, carried her haunch through the pines. In my head his action played out like a song, *country separated from continent, long walk home.*

9.

When grandma died, someone thought I should have a journal—my first language lesson. I could hardly write, so much so, I didn't understand the necessity of putting spaces between words. *But why?* I asked. *So people can understand you.* And in those absences I grew a meaning—

Jettison

Each year she hovered
the yahrzeit flame,
shadows riding the fibers
of her song as she
prayed for her
mother's ascent.

Yitbarach

v'yishtabach v'yitpaar

v'yitromam v'yitnasei,

v'yit'hadar v'yitaleh

v'yit'halal

sh'mei d'Kud'sha B'richu

which means

blessed and praised,

glorified and exalted,

extolled and honored,

adored and lauded be the name

of the Holy One, blessed be He,

beyond all the blessings and hymns,

praises and consolations

that are ever spoken

in the world; and say, Amen.

But those of us in the room didn't

know the meaning,

just that there was a mother

before this mother,

that prayer can

mean *honor* and

there is nothing I can say

to reach you.

*

A song for the dead is a song for the mourners,

the voice a primordial cord, pulling.

Blessed, praised, honored, exalted,

extolled, glorified, adored, and lauded be the name

of the Holy Blessed One,

beyond all earthly words and songs

of blessing, praise, and comfort.

To which we say: Amen.

I like this iteration best—

earthly words,

and beyond them,

other words unearthly.

Praise the voice, the mind's articulation.

When my grandmother lost her voice

to a stroke she reduced to sound, movement,

instrumental song—

this was the first passage

toward transmigration.

　　Where does language go when

the body keeps on living?

　　And if I say it burrows in the marrow,

will you say, *amen?*

　　And if I say it vanishes

　　will you say, *amen?*

If my grandmother can't speak

the Kaddish, will my great-grandmother's

soul keep on traveling—

the price of formlessness?

And if I say that every articulation

　　　　　of the body is the prayer? (she took to waving her hands

after each meal, pushing back on the glass table, to say *I'm finished,* not thinking

about how little it would take for the large pane to slip from its base to shatter, that

she constantly pushed her body away from things)—

　　　　　　　would you hearken?

*

The grief of wordlessness casts

my mother wordless sometimes—

　　can a song resurrect

in that absence?

*

It could have been like this—
first, the slowing of the blood,
where her right brain
eased toward her left,
and left toward the right,
two floating jackfruit contained in
the ivory of her skull,
like lovers who do not touch,
but speak in holier intimacy:
all heat-current and vein.
That maybe her dying cells aimed skyward,
leaving behind their minute bodies
as golden isles traversing all the channels,
spindrift and wild, weightlessness
taking on new weightlessness—
their collective loyalty to the body
a thing of the past, and she
halving for years before her
own ascent.

Never mind her voice,
Never mind her dexterity.
The brain, the body are a mystery.
I try to tell my mother
all I know, things I've read here and there.
That perhaps my grandmother,
all soft and right-brained,
lived in a new world,
impeccably drawn for her—

My grandfather enters the room,

the tumble of our voices,

our reaching hands,

the flowers and their translucent stems

all wondrous meridians from which to feast.

*

When I leave home,

I don't know that I am making a trade—

one birthplace for the next,

I keep the travel prayer

a friend gave me, use it as a bookmark

and an elegy.

May it be Your will, G–d, our G–d and the G–d

of our fathers, that You should lead us in peace

and direct our steps in peace, and guide us in peace,

and support us in peace, and cause us to reach our

destination in life, joy, and peace

(If one intends to return soon, one adds: and return us in peace).

Your eyes and in the eyes of all who see us,

and bestow upon us abundant kindness and hearken

to the voice of our prayer, for You hear the prayers

of all. Blessed are You G–d, who hearkens to prayer.

What to call her without a voice for so many years

—body, grandmother, movement,
instrument, song.

A being can exist among two
(or more) planes, can be in a constant state
of becoming. This is
leaving, I think.

    I did not pray
    until death sounded, and finally,
    I hearkened.

*

At her shiva we feast on
nuts and fruit, bread to honor
the labor of her body and ours.
In the sunroom men pray for her
soul's ascent, the Hebrew I can't help
but mouth, surfaces—
again, the mourner's prayer,
but I have brought with me the travel song

(If one intends to return soon, one adds: and return us in peace)
    Who is here in the room?

Who are you,
elongated shadow
casting yourself obviously on the lawn?

(If one intends to return soon, one adds: and return us in peace)

Birdsong, bee-hum accompanies the echoed
voices in the room.

What aria of light trembles its perfect
percussion on our flesh?

*

Now I have two grandmothers traveling.

When I was a child
my other grandmother
traveled a great distance
through air to
go die in her birthplace,
knowing
her body would be cast to fire,
then water—

How does one look down
at their hands in their lap and not
already see their shadow there
pooling in the hollow?
Who were we,
small on the ground,
as the large craft holding her body pushed
through sky?

How much mourning does it take
to reshape the air?
What prayer do the dying sing for themselves?

In my memory, this grandma articulates
in storm sounds. She gathers me.

Disease hasn't yet split
the seedcase
of her skin, but tonight the storm
splits the silver casing of the sky
and calls it giving—
uncoiling again and again back
into itself, its loud talk ricocheting off the trees,
cresting in our bodies—mine trembling. And at
the second-story window, my grandma
opens it to feel the storm,
to not be afraid of what rages.
The storm sucks the screen in and back,
metallic, charged, damp taking and giving the
smell of the backyard lawn which tries to absorb
the rain. Lightning cracks the childhood
elm, one year later it will die of beetle-kill
but tonight its singed bark sings back.
I shudder and my grandmother,
singing in my eardrum, says, *tomorrow everything,*
will be greener—
which I hear as:

we do not know yet what will come

while we sleep, all the shimmering aspects:

the possibility of tomorrow's bulb of sun,

tiny pool in the seat of my swing,

and from the depths of the black-eyed flower, seed,

translucent dividends born to split

the air, to travel on and on

questing and unseen.

The Body of the Guru

A bustling airport, my aunt pulls up an app
called *myguru,* tells me everyday she reads

ten pages of scripture—*every line is Hindi
Punjabi and English,* she says of the words aglow

behind the glass, then confesses her wish
that my grandmother were still here to teach me.

What steadiness it takes to write the word of god,
to imbue spirit into paper, an app. I recall

the book *The Making of a Sikh Scripture* where the author
uses language like *clothe this revelation* and *the body of the guru.*

The big question: *Many ask, if the children
do not inherit the tradition, then how will it*

survive in foreign lands? What devotion—
from belief, to scribe, to pages, to printing press,

to silken robes, the body. I once asked
my father how many letters are in the Hindi alphabet

and he said I should look it up.
Didn't you go to school? I joked. *I just*

can't remember. Over the PA a voice announces
our departures so my aunt and I head out
our separate gates.

Why I ask for you to come in dreams

because the first time, you were a
replica of before, the avenues

of grief split open like a fist, my synapses charged
and hot.

Because the second time I found you.
Your sleek composition hidden in a wetfield

sprung up from the mouth of an oyster,
lean, translucent grass, saying, *wind swept me this way.*

Because the last time I saw you in this life
you confessed your desire to change shape,

drought body, stagnant landscape—
I'm tired of this.

Because sometimes at night
I can't shake how a body can own and then

disown its form.

The third time, in dream: *do you know the stones
are listening even though they are dead?*

What We Believed

Once, we spent an entire evening talking ourselves out
of the idea

that language really mattered,

yet a week later, there we were, with words strewn across
notebooks,

and paintings,
the fire hissing hungry. You said, *ritual,* begged

for a *cleansing,* threw your language
into the fire's mouth, which only made it grow louder,

and only made us think harder
about the smoke rising, how it looked like luxurious script

spelling out our separate
desires, and in the end,

the paper down to its pieces, reduced, but still
there, teaching us something about
the ineffable.

On Absence

My grandfather was not sent off to fight
but assigned to deliver news of the dead.

The glass doors separated him from them—
mothers saw his uniformed approach

and he saw, before the turn of the handle,
the way grief contorts the face so sharply,

it's hard to believe in a life separate
from the bone.

Decades later, after his funeral, we filled his house.
The living room so cluttered with matter—

silver platters of food, couches, serious chairs,
columns, skylights, bodies—

and without trying, I felt him,
woven from the benign and opaque.

Magic isn't right, neither is *epiphany.*

He was a speech professor after the war,
teaching students to carve emphasis out of

language so something unnamable could take shape.
Maybe it was something like that—

how fingers are not dissimilar from wands,
the way I could have pointed to the air

and said *there he is—*

Notes on the Amorphous

After she died, I was sent (again)
to sit upright. For weeks, stricken, hung,
all splinter and bone, I sat. I tried to write her

but didn't know where to start—
her body or the velvet timbre
to her fall, as I tried not to consider it.
Weeks go by and finally I succumbed:

Ok, fine, there are limits to language.
Outside the day is clear, so I read a book
that says *amber* so many times
I think maybe I'd written this book

already: *Every precious resin . . . its own peculiar virtue.*
Listen: I've learned to let the world divine her,
I've put the paper down, and when she
comes to me in the vast places

I hear her refrain:
someday I'll be a stone,
that ordinary stagnant, weight.

After Watching *Religulous* With a Friend

Shaken, my friend tells me she's spent her entire life inside the church's walls,
  doesn't know what to make of the movie that refuses to indulge a made-up god,

says she hasn't spent much time, until now, thinking about faiths outside
  her own. In the movie, Rabbis bow in rapid succession, priests claim to take

on the supernatural ability to cure all ailments, and all the monotheistic religions agree:
  one god, out there, watching. There are words I could use to tell her

I mostly agree—all of it a ridiculous display, wars fought, that ever since
  I was a child I've practiced writing myself out. I'm not saying we should replace

god with *art* or am I? I want to find the words to say that I think there are many ways to
  surrender–how we've spent years going to this theater, escaped

the bright lobby to go silhouette among narratives unlike our own—remember the one
  from last week? The woman digging through dirt as if she'd find the piece of her

life that went missing? The ray of light that pooled for us?
  How we believed it was designed for us?

Book Arts

In the beginning there were the raw materials:
paper, ink, thread and glue. There were books
to help the class make books. *What is a book?*
intros asked and so many different forms:
accordion books, fold books, signature books.
We'll start by talking about the body of the book,
the teacher said. The diagram showed a traditional
book with the head, spine, tail front board,
and back board. The book asked, *How do we define a page?*

*

It was snowing. I saw you thread the needle
and pierce the pages. I saw you build a book.
I saw you use your hands. It all begins with blank pages—
a thrilling absence. I could use my hands while
across the room you used your hands.
I saw you weave an intricate binding.

*

At home, I ponder the assignment: to build a
home-themed book. I print vintage maps of my
city, trace the familiar avenues with my finger,
cut them off. The roof will contain pages using
a simple saddle stitching, the body will be filled
with tiny photographs of homepeople,
notes about elms and buckeyes,
and odes to city benches.

*

You build a scroll that can be seen
from the window of its casing.
You rotate it for the class,
the moving images of hand mudras.

*

It was snowing in the high desert.
We spent weeks inside the
classroom. Then we were taking walks,
leaving our supplies,
crisp spines of paper gaping.
Bone folders.

*

You could say that on the drying rack sat
the empty bodies, that the form cast the meaning.
Some were so immaculate and well-produced
it appeared that a machine had made them.

*

I learn to leave the pages blank,
that a book can be so many things,
like the book I built by shatter.
Each glass shard had a letter
and was suspended in a jar of water,
just to see the alphabet floating
away from meaning.

*

You took me to a juniper tree
that sheltered a rock from snow.
We exchanged small pieces
of language. There were pulpy pieces
of paper in your hair,
snowflakes.
I didn't want our meeting
to articulate in winter,
the cold month, the blank landscape.
Each day our footsteps to and from
our books, punctuating snow.

Inflorescence

On our first date, you asked me about the woods
        of my childhood, my thoughts on god.

We both agreed that it was a complicated question and
        a simple one.

Then we were picking flowers, pressing their benign
        weight between pages. In the days

we waited, I showed you a small, handmade
        book, one I loved for how easy it seemed

to put together. You told me if you take two pieces of clear
        tape, the flowers would be preserved.

Some stems had broken off, and some leaves were more
        beautiful than other leaves, so we placed

flower heads with other stems, leaves with other
        flower heads, and pressed.

Casting, Pulling

You tell me you make your own runes—
first you collect,
then you carve the symbol.
You use words on me,
words like *engrave, divine.*
Look, you say, casting the stones
smoothly over the table's surface.
Close your eyes and feel.

I learn to choose.
We are three weeks old—
I want to pull the stone
that will tell me all about
love's believing,
that will articulate the process
of pulling, the way you
pulled pebbles from beneath
the water's skin
because they felt right.

If you took out the e, you could be like the stream,

the woman behind the counter says.

And for a moment, a new way

of being: I could be the Grand Stream and every bright

nutrient would bloat my cells so when people drank

they too would grow golden.

I'd be sure to flow at just the right speed

so when visitors came to rest along

my shore, they'd be reminded,

gently, of keeping a steady pace.

More than likely

it would be one of those subtle, but ultimately

significant changes, the way a river rock

rearranged forms new braids of water

and this discourse affects the flow of the

communal body.

Truth is, I hate the way my name looks

on the page without the e, like part

of me is missing,

masculine, so far from water.

Outside, Eerie exhales large-frothed breaths

to the shore as the sky goes mauve, to purple,

to black. God is g–d is god.

I call it stormcloud,

unforeseeable potential

to come down—

or not—to wet us until we seek

cover, silken, or go on walking.

Ritual, Begging

Because it involves water and want.
Ritual says, *come-rid-yourself-a-cleansing.*

I have tried to ritual things for myself,
and yet. Because the Jewish New Year

always falls in autumn and it is plain
to see the water's pull.

Because it's uncomfortable
in the body to have old ideas

and nowhere to place them. Ritual says,
don't look at what is obstructed

and *all is flowing naturally.* I contemplate
the difference between what I want

to cast away and what I want
to pull in. In my hand,

the bread, the blank page. I've
come to this shore and I will

again. Because if I listen, I hear it.
Ritual says, *Didn't you know the river's hunger*

is insatiable
and it all goes to the same place anyway?

The Golden Reserve

*Seeing Thy supremely beautiful form, and hearing the musical tinkling of Thy silver
bells. . . .* Under his breath my dad mutters, *soothing, soothing.*

There is majesty in the Michigan fields, so far-reaching they undulate with the iPod's
prayers. We're not supposed to talk, but every so often my aunt leans in

to translate for me. It's not the Ganges, but my aunt had done her homework—no
regulations here. Last night my cousin and I unearthed

a slim, pink exercise notepad labeled, "Harmeet's recipe book." First, the initial laugh—a
man who never ceased to love food, wrote himself a chronicle of sweets.

Upstairs, a fridge stands still of insulin, liters of Coke line the walls, hoards of coriander,
wadi, garam masala for next time.

We will get into the car and not speak until we reach the river, my aunt instructs.
People have always told me I have my grandmother's hands,

my father's are two ghosts gripping the bag. *Snowy Boiled Frosting: 2 cups sugar
2 cups water dash of salt 2 egg whites combine.*

Yesterday at the crematorium my father confessed: *I don't want to press the button,* and
after *what quick efficiency.* Oh, the full bodies of cakes: delicious

date nut bread, orange lemon funnel cake, black moon pudding, because
I want to think of fat,

alive, wobbling, the pleasure of food and not the measured portions.
Sea Foam Frosting with two cups of brown sugar packed down.

The weight of the world. Weathered barns, leather-coated steering wheel, the bag
on my father's lap that looks like a present.

I took the *Karah Prasad* and ate it, it stuck to my mouth like a second layer of flesh.
I couldn't speak and there was nothing to say anyway. The Gurdwara glittered.

It's no exaggeration to say I saw the body's particles shimmer on the water
like a trout, go cumulous, gold to blue.

*Monogram Pancakes: with a teaspoon of batter, outline initials on the griddle
then pour batter over and surround the letters until golden.*

Forgive me but there is no clean way to dispose of a body,
        because the body collects and stores. The river reeds tremble

and can only do so much to rectify what we're about to give them.
        I need to say thank you, uncle. I watched you enjoy, enjoy, enjoy.

Acknowledgments

The Journal	. . .	"Why I ask for you to come in dreams"
Interim Poetics	. . .	"Inflorescence"
		"Casting, Pulling"
Prairie Schooner	. . .	"Before I had the word"
		"Heritage Day"
		"On Absence"
Nimrod International Journal	. . .	"The Golden Reserve"
		"What My Mother Knows"
Cimarron Review	. . .	"Natural Law,"
	. . .	"To the girl who cried over grass"
The Missouri Review Poem of the Week	. . .	"The Body of the Guru"
Tinderbox Poetry Journal	. . .	"Notes on Midrash"
The Massachusetts Review	. . .	"G-d, a Portrait"
Spillway	. . .	"Notes on the Amorphous"
EcoTheo Review	. . .	"Reform"
32 Poems	. . .	"Language Lesson"
Superstition Review	. . .	"Whose Kingdom"
	. . .	"Leaving a Scripture"
Denver Quarterly	. . .	"If you took out the *e*, you could be like the stream"
River Styx	. . .	"*Mangifera Indica*"
The Cincinnati Review	. . .	"After Watching *Religulous* with a Friend"
The Shore	. . .	"*The Sensuous Woman* by J"

The 2019 Orison Chapbook Prize